Poems from the First World War

Gaby Morgan has edited a number of bestselling anthologies, including *Read Me and Laugh: A Funny Poem for Every Day of the Year* and *Christmas Poems*.

The Imperial War Museum was founded in 1917 to collect and display material relating to the First World War, which was still being fought. Today IWM is unique in its coverage of conflicts, especially those involving Britain and the Commonwealth, from the First World War to the present. It seeks to provide for, and to encourage, the study and understanding of the history of modern war and wartime experience.

In Association with IWM

Poems from the First World War

Selected by
Gaby Morgan

MACMILLAN CHILDREN'S BOOKS

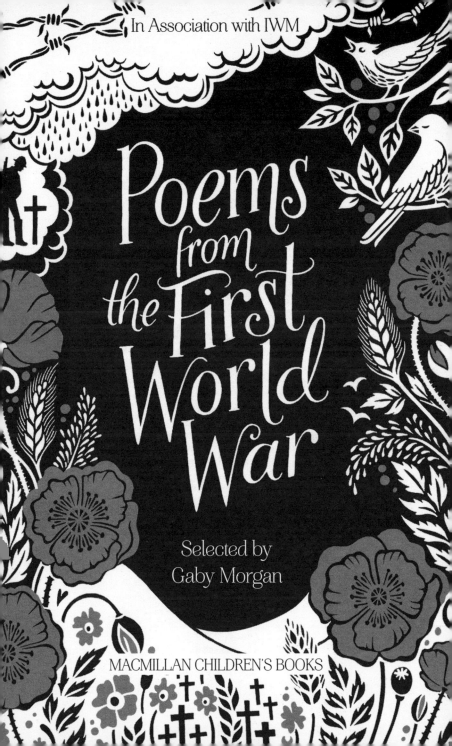

First published 2013 by Macmillan Children's Books
a division of Macmillan Publishers Limited
20 New Wharf Road, London N1 9RR
Basingstoke and Oxford
Associated companies throughout the world
www.panmacmillan.com

ISBN 978-1-4472-5651-9

1 3 5 7 9 8 6 4 2

A CIP catalogue record for this book is available from
the British Library.

Typeset by Kate Warren
Printed and bound by CPI Group (UK) Ltd, Croydon CR0 4YY

iwm.org.uk

*For Polly Nolan, Suzanne Carnell
and Jackie McCann*

Contents

ENGLAND TO HER SONS

Sons of mine, I hear you thrilling
To the trumpet call of war;
Gird ye then, I give you freely
As I gave your sires before,
All the noblest of the children I in love and
    anguish bore.

Free in service, wise in justice,
Fearing but dishonour's breath;
Steeled to suffer uncomplaining
Loss and failure, pain and death;
Strong in faith that sees the issue and in hope that
    triumpheth.

Go, and may the God of battles
You in His good guidance keep:
And if He in wisdom giveth
Unto His beloved sleep,
I accept it nothing asking, save a little space to
    weep.

W. N. Hodgson
Written in August 1914

GLIMPSE

I saw you fooling often in the tents
With fair dishevelled hair and laughing lips,
And frolic elf lights in your careless eyes,
As who had never known the taste of tears
Or the world's sorrow. Then on the march
  one night,
Halted beneath the stars I heard the sound
Of talk and laughter, and glanced back to see
If you were there. But you stood far apart
And silent, bowed upon your rifle butt,
And gazed into the night as one who sees.
I marked the drooping lips and fathomless eyes
And knew you brooded on immortal things.

W. N. Hodgson
Written in June 1914

from MEN WHO MARCH AWAY

In our heart of hearts believing
    Victory crowns the just,
    And that braggarts must
    Surely bite the dust,
Press we to the field ungrieving,
In our heart of hearts believing
    Victory crowns the just.

Hence the faith and fire within us
    Men who march away
    Ere the barn-cocks say
    Night is growing gray,
Leaving all that here can win us;
Hence the faith and fire within us
    Men who march away.

Thomas Hardy
September 1914

Happy Is England Now

There is not anything more wonderful
Than a great people moving towards the deep
Of an unguessed and unfeared future; nor
Is aught so dear of all held dear before
As the new passion stirring in their veins
When the destroying dragon wakes from sleep.

Happy is England now, as never yet!
And though the sorrows of the slow days fret
Her faithfullest children, grief itself is proud.
Ev'n the warm beauty of this spring and summer
That turns to bitterness turns then to gladness
Since for this England the beloved ones died.

Happy is England in the brave that die
For wrongs not hers and wrongs so sternly hers;
Happy in those that give, give, and endure
The pain that never the new years may cure;
Happy in all her dark woods, green fields, towns,
Her hills and rivers and her chafing sea.

Whate'er was dear before is dearer now.
There's not a bird singing upon this bough
But sings the sweeter in our English ears:
There's not a nobleness of heart, hand, brain,
But shines the purer; happiest is England now
In those that fight, and watch with pride and tears.

John Freeman
1914

BEFORE ACTION

By all the glories of the day
And the cool evening's benison,
By that last sunset touch that lay
Upon the hills when day was done,
By beauty lavishly outpoured
And blessings carelessly received,
By all the days that I have lived
Make me a soldier, Lord.

By all of man's hopes and fears,
And all the wonders poets sing,
The laughter of unclouded years,
And every sad and lovely thing;
By the romantic ages stored
With high endeavour that was his,
By all his mad catastrophes
Make me a man, O Lord.

I, that on my familiar hill
Saw with uncomprehending eyes
A hundred of Thy sunsets spill
Their fresh and sanguine sacrifice,
Ere the sun swings his noonday sword
Must say goodbye to all of this; –
By all delights that I shall miss,
Help me to die, O Lord.

W. N. Hodgson

THE CALL

Who's for the trench –
Are you, my laddie?
Who'll follow French –
Will you, my laddie?
Who's fretting to begin,
Who's going out to win?
And who wants to save his skin –
Do you, my laddie?

Who's for the khaki suit –
Are you, my laddie?
Who longs to charge and shoot –
Do you, my laddie?
Who's keen on getting fit,
Who means to show his grit,
And who'd rather wait a bit –
Would you, my laddie?

Who'll earn the Empire's thanks –
Will you, my laddie?
Who'll swell the victor's ranks –
Will you, my laddie?
When that procession comes,
Banners and rolling drums –
Who'll stand and bite his thumbs –
Will you, my laddie?

Jessie Pope

DRILLING IN RUSSELL SQUARE

The withered leaves that drift in Russell Square
Will turn to mud and dust and moulder there
And we shall moulder in the plains of France
Before these leaves have ceased from their
   last dance.
The hot sun triumphs through the fading trees,
The fading houses keep away the breeze
And the autumnal warmth strange dreams
   doth breed
As right and left the faltering columns lead.
Squad, 'shun! Form fours . . . And once the France
   we knew
Was a warm distant place with sun shot through,
A happy land of gracious palaces,
And Paris! Paris! Where twice green the trees
Do twice salute the all delightful year!
(Though the sun lives, the trees are dying here.)
And Germany we thought a singing place,
Where in the hamlets dwelt a simple race,
Where th' untaught villager would still compose
Delicious things upon a girl or rose.
Well, I suppose all I shall see of France

Will be most clouded by an Uhlan's lance,
Red fields from cover glimpsed be all I see
Of innocent, singing, peasant Germany.

Form-four-rs! Form two deep! We wheel and pair
And still the brown leaves drift in Russell Square.

Edward Shanks

GOING IN TO DINNER

Beat the knife on the plate and the fork on the can,
For we're going in to dinner, so make all the noise
   you can,
Up and down the officer wanders, looking blue,
Sing a song to cheer him up, he wants his dinner too.

March into the village-school, make the tables rattle
Like a dozen dam' machine-guns in the bloody-
   battle,
Use your forks for drumsticks, use your plates for
   drums,
Make a most infernal clatter, here the dinner comes!

Edward Shanks

THE CALL

Ah! we have dwelt in Arcady long time
  With sun and youth eternal round our ways
And in the magic of that golden clime
  We loved the pageant of the passing days.

The wonderful white dawns of frost and flame
  In winter, and the swift sun's upward leap;
Or summer's stealthy wakening that came
  Soft as a whisper on the lips of sleep.

And there were woodland hollows of green lawn,
  Where boys with windy hair and wine wet lips
Danced on the sun-splashed grass; and hills of
                                        dawn
  That looked out seaward to the distant ships.

In infinite still night the moon swam low
  And saffron in a silver dusted sky;
Beauty and sorrow hand in hand with slow
  Soft wings and soundless passage wandered by.

And white roads vanishing beneath the sky
  Called for our feet, and there were countless
                                    things
That we must see and do, while blood was high
  And time still hovered on reluctant wings.

And these were good; yet in our hearts we knew
  These were not all, – that still through toil and
                                    pains
Deeds of a purer lustre given to few,
  Made for the perfect glory that remains.

And when the summons in our ears was shrill
  Unshaken in our trust we rose, and then
Flung but a backward glance, and care-free still
  Went strongly forth to do the work of men.

W. N. Hodgson

THE SEND-OFF

Down the close, darkening lanes they sang their way
To the siding-shed,
And lined the train with faces grimly gay.

Their breasts were stuck all white with wreath and
    spray
As men's are, dead.

Dull porters watched them, and a casual tramp
Stood staring hard,
Sorry to miss them from the upland camp.
Then, unmoved, signals nodded, and a lamp
Winked to the guard.

So secretly, like wrongs hushed-up, they went.
They were not ours:
We never heard to which front these were sent.

Nor there if they yet mock what women meant
Who gave them flowers.

Shall they return to beatings of great bells
In wild trainloads?
A few, a few, too few for drums and yells,
May creep back, silent, to still village wells
Up half-known roads.

Wilfred Owen

THE SOLDIER

If I should die, think only this of me:
   That there's some corner of a foreign field
That is for ever England. There shall be
   In that rich earth a richer dust concealed;
A dust whom England bore, shaped, made aware,
   Gave, once, her flowers to love, her ways to roam,
A body of England's, breathing English air,
   Washed by the rivers, blest by suns of home.

And think, this heart, all evil shed away,
   A pulse in the eternal mind, no less
     Gives somewhere back the thoughts by England
                     given;
Her sights and sounds; dreams happy as her day;
   And laughter, learnt of friends; and gentleness,
     In hearts at peace, under an English heaven.

Rupert Brooke

On Receiving News of the War

Snow is a strange white word;
No ice or frost
Have asked of bud or bird
For Winter's cost.

Yet ice and frost and snow
From earth to sky
This Summer land doth know,
No man knows why.

In all men's hearts it is.
Some spirit old
Hath turned with malign kiss
Our lives to mould.

Red fangs have torn His face.
God's blood is shed.
He mourns from His lone place
His children dead.

O! ancient crimson curse!
Corrode, consume.
Give back this universe
Its pristine bloom.

Isaac Rosenberg
Cape Town, 1914

BREAKFAST

We ate our breakfast lying on our backs,
Because the shells were screeching overhead.
I bet a rasher to a loaf of bread
That Hull United would beat Halifax
When Jimmy Stainthorp played full-back instead
Of Billy Bradford. Ginger raised his head
And cursed, and took the bet; and dropt back
    dead.
We ate our breakfast lying on our backs,
Because the shells were screeching overhead.

W. W. Gibson
Published in October 1914

Peace

Now, God be thanked Who has matched us with
   His hour,
And caught our youth and wakened us from sleeping,
With hand made sure, clear eye, and sharpened
   power,
To turn, as swimmers into cleanness leaping,
Glad from a world grown old and cold and weary,
Leave the sick hearts that honour could not move,
And half-men, and their dirty songs and dreary,
And all the little emptiness of love!

Oh! we who have known shame, we have found
   release there,
Where there's no ill, no grief, but sleep has mending,
Naught broken save this body, lost but breath;
Nothing to shake the laughing heart's long peace
   there
But only agony, and that has ending;
And the worst friend and enemy is but Death.

Rupert Brooke
Written in December 1914

For the Fallen

With proud thanksgiving, a mother for her children,
England mourns for her dead across the sea.
Flesh of her flesh they were, spirit of her spirit,
Fallen in the cause of the free.

Solemn the drums thrill: Death august and royal
Sings sorrow up into immortal spheres.
There is music in the midst of desolation
And a glory that shines upon our tears.

They went with songs to the battle, they were young,
Straight of limb, true of eye, steady and aglow.
They were staunch to the end against odds
    uncounted,
They fell with their faces to the foe.

They shall grow not old, as we that are left grow old:
Age shall not weary them, nor the years condemn.
At the going down of the sun and in the morning
We will remember them.

They mingle not with their laughing comrades again;
They sit no more at familiar tables of home;
They have no lot in our labour of the day-time;
They sleep beyond England's foam.

But where our desires are and our hopes profound,
Felt as a well-spring that is hidden from sight,
To the innermost heart of their own land they are
   known
As the stars are known to the Night;

As the stars that shall be bright when we are dust,
Moving in marches upon the heavenly plain,
As the stars that are starry in the time of our darkness,
To the end, to the end, they remain.

Laurence Binyon
September 1914

The Dead

These hearts were woven of human joys and cares,
  Washed marvellously with sorrow, swift to mirth.
The years had given them kindness. Dawn was theirs,
  And sunset, and the colours of the earth.
These had seen movement, and heard music; known
  Slumber and waking; loved; gone proudly friended;
Felt the quick stir of wonder; sat alone;
  Touched flowers and furs and cheeks. All this is
                                             ended.

There are waters blown by changing winds to
                                          laughter
And lit by the rich skies, all day. And after,
  Frost, with a gesture, stays the waves that dance
And wandering loveliness. He leaves a white
  Unbroken glory, a gathered radiance,
A width, a shining peace, under the night

Rupert Brooke
1914

MANGEL-WURZELS

Last year I was hoeing,
Hoeing mangel-wurzels,
Hoeing mangel-wurzels all day in the sun,
Hoeing for the squire
Down in Gloucestershire,
Willy-nilly till the sweaty job was done.

Now I'm in the 'wurzels,
In the mangel-wurzels,
All day in the 'wurzels 'neath the Belgian sun:
But among this little lot
It's a different job I've got—
For you don't hoe mangel-wurzels with a gun.

W. W. Gibson

THE VOLUNTEER

Here lies a clerk who half his life had spent
Toiling at ledgers in a city grey,
Thinking that so his days would drift away
With no lance broken in life's tournament.
Yet ever 'twixt the books and his bright eyes
The gleaming eagles of the legions came,
And horsemen, charging under phantom skies,
Went thundering past beneath the oriflamme.

And now those waiting dreams are satisfied;
From twilight to the halls of dawn he went;
His lance is broken; but he lies content
With that high hour, in which he lived and died.
And falling thus he wants no recompense,
Who found his battle in the last resort;
Nor need he any hearse to bear him hence,
Who goes to join the men of Agincourt.

Herbert Asquith

Field Manoeuvres

Outpost Duty

The long autumn grass under my body
Soaks my clothes with its dew;
Where my knees press into the ground
I can feel the damp earth.

In my nostrils is the smell of the crushed grass,
Wet pine-cones and bark.

Through the great bronze pine trunks
Glitters a silver segment of road.
Interminable squadrons of silver and blue horses
Pace in long ranks the blank fields of heaven.

There is no sound;
The wind hisses gently through the pine needles;
The flutter of a finch's wings about my head
Is like distant thunder,
And the shrill cry of a mosquito
Sounds loud and close.

I am 'to fire at the enemy column
After it has passed' –
But my obsolete rifle, loaded with 'blank',
Lies untouched before me,
My spirit follows after the gliding clouds,
And my lips murmur of the mother of beauty
Standing breast-high, in golden broom
Among the blue pine-woods!

Richard Aldington

From a Flemish Graveyard

A year hence may the grass that waves
O'er English men in Flemish graves,
Coating this clay with green of peace
And softness of a year's increase,
Be kind and lithe as English grass
To bend and nod as the winds pass;
It was for grass on English hills
These bore too soon the last of ills.

And may the wind be brisk and clean,
And singing cheerfully between
The bents a pleasant-burdened song
To cheer these English dead along;
For English songs and English winds
Are they that bred these English minds.

And may the circumstantial trees
Dip, for these dead ones, in the breeze,
And make for them their silver play
Of spangled boughs each shiny day.
Thus may these look above, and see
And hear the wind in grass and tree,
And watch a lark in heaven stand,
And think themselves in their own land.

I. A. Williams

FLANDERS

Man has the life of butterflies
In the sunshine of sacrifice;
Brief and brilliant, but more
Guerdon than the honeyed flower,
And more glory than the grace
Of their gentle floating pace.

Willoughby Weaving

THE CHERRY TREES

The cherry trees bend over and are shedding
On the old road where all that passed are dead,
Their petals, strewing the grass as for a wedding
This early May morn when there is none to wed.

Edward Thomas

MARCHING (AS SEEN FROM THE LEFT FILE)

My eyes catch ruddy necks
Sturdily pressed back –
All a red brick moving glint.
Like flaming pendulums, hands
Swing across the khaki –
Mustard-coloured khaki –
To the automatic feet.
We husband the ancient glory
In these bared necks and hands.
Not broke is the forge of Mars;
But a subtler brain beats iron
To shoe the hoofs of death,
(Who paws dynamic air now).
Blind fingers loose an iron cloud
To rain immortal darkness
On strong eyes.

Isaac Rosenberg

NOON

It is midday: the deep trench glares . . .
A buzz and blaze of flies . . .
The hot wind puffs the giddy airs . . .
The great sun rakes the skies.

No sound in all the stagnant trench
Where forty standing men
Endure the sweat and grit and stench,
Like cattle in a pen.

Sometimes a sniper's bullet whirs
Or twangs the whining wire,
Sometimes a soldier sighs and stirs
As in hell's frying fire.

From out a high cool cloud descends
An aeroplane's far moan . . .
The sun strikes down, the thin cloud rends . . .
The black spot travels on.

And sweating, dizzied, isolate
In the hot trench beneath,
We bide the next shrewd move of fate
Be it of life or death.

Robert Nichols

THE FALLING LEAVES

Today, as I rode by,
I saw the brown leaves dropping from their tree
In a still afternoon,
When no wind whirled them whistling to the sky,
But thickly, silently,
They fell, like snowflakes wiping out the noon;
And wandered slowly thence
For thinking of a gallant multitude
Which now all withering lay,
Slain by no wind of age or pestilence,
But in their beauty strewed
Like snowflakes falling on the Flemish clay.

Margaret Postgate Cole
November 1915

'MY BOY JACK' 1914–18

'Have you news of my boy Jack?'
Not this tide.
'When d'you think that he'll come back?'
Not with this wind blowing, and this tide.

'Has any one else had word of him?'
Not this tide.
For what is sunk will hardly swim,
Not with this wind blowing, and this tide.

'Oh, dear, what comfort can I find?'
None this tide,
Nor any tide,
Except he did not shame his kind—
Not even with that wind blowing, and that tide.

Then hold your head up all the more,
This tide,
And every tide;
Because he was the son you bore,
And gave to that wind blowing and that tide.

Rudyard Kipling

A Son

My son was killed while laughing at some jest. I
would I knew
What it was, and it might serve me in a time when
jests are few.

Rudyard Kipling

'WHEN YOU SEE MILLIONS OF THE MOUTHLESS DEAD'

When you see millions of the mouthless dead
Across your dreams in pale battalions go,
Say not soft things as other men have said,
That you'll remember. For you need not so.
Give them not praise. For, deaf, how should they
   know
It is not curses heaped on each gashed head?
Nor tears. Their blind eyes see not your tears flow.
Nor honour. It is easy to be dead.
Say only this, 'They are dead.' Then add thereto,
'Yet many a better one has died before.'
Then, scanning all the o'ercrowded mass, should you
Perceive one face that you loved heretofore,
It is a spook. None wears the face you knew.
Great death has made all his for evermore.

Charles Sorley
Written in 1915

BACK

They ask me where I've been,
And what I've done and seen.
But what can I reply
Who know it wasn't I,
But someone just like me,
Who went across the sea
And with my head and hands
Killed men in foreign lands . . .
Though I must bear the blame,
Because he bore my name.

W. W. Gibson
Published in July 1915

A LISTENING POST

The sun's a red ball in the oak
And all the grass is grey with dew,
A while ago a blackbird spoke –
He didn't know the world's askew

And yonder rifleman and I
Wait here behind the misty trees
To shoot the first man that goes by,
Our rifles ready on our knees.

How could he know that if we fail
The world may lie in chains for years
And England be a bygone tale
And right be wrong, and laughter tears?

Strange that this bird sits there and sings
While we must only sit and plan –
Who are so much the higher thing –
The murder of our fellow man . . .

But maybe God will cause to be –
Who brought forth sweetness from the strong –
Out of our discords harmony
Sweeter than the bird's song.

R. E. Vernède
Written before March 1915

ANNIVERSARY OF THE GREAT RETREAT
(1915)

Now a whole year has waxed and waned and
>> whitened
> Over the mounds that marked that grim
>> advance;
The winter snows have lain, the spring flowers
>> brightened,
> On those belovèd graves of Northern France.

Caudry, Le Cateau, Landrécies, are written
> In our sad hearts with letters as of flame,
Where our young dead still lie, untimely smitten,
> In graves still unredeemed that bear no name.

And those who saw them spoke of the 'boy-faces'
> The English soldiers wore; they heard them sing
As they went forth to their appointed places,
> Who when night fell lay unremembering. . . .

O England, sing their fame in song and story,
> Who knew Death's victory not Life's defeat;
Be their names written on thy roll of glory,
> Who fought and perished in the Great Retreat!

These held thy high tradition in their keeping
   This flower of all a nation's youth and pride
And safe they hold it still in their last sleeping;
   They heard thy call and answered it and died. . . .

And by those graves that mark their proud
                               surrender
   In days to come each one that lingereth
Shall sadly think of all their vanished splendour,
   'Contemptible', but faithful unto death.

So we press forward, step by step redeeming
   Each hallowed spot our dead have sanctified,
That we may whisper to them in their dreaming,
   The Victory is ours because you died. . . .

Isabel C. Clarke

FLANDERS FIELDS

Here the scanted daisy glows
Glorious as the carmined rose;
Here the hill-top's verdure mean
Fair is with unfading green;
Here, where sorrow still must tread,
All her graves are garlanded.

And still, O glad passer-by
Of the fields of agony,
Lower laughter's voice, and bare
Thy head in the valley where
Poppies bright and rustling wheat
Are a desert to love's feet.

Elizabeth Daryush

THE DESERTER

There was a man, – don't mind his name,
Whom Fear had dogged by night and day.
He could not face the German guns
And so he turned and ran away.
Just that – he turned and ran away,
But who can judge him, you or I?
God makes a man of flesh and blood
Who yearns to live and not to die.
And this man when he feared to die
Was scared as any frightened child,
His knees were shaking under him,
His breath came fast, his eyes were wild.
I've seen a hare with eyes as wild,
With throbbing heart and sobbing breath.
But oh! it shames one's soul to see
A man in abject fear of death.
But fear had gripped him, so had death;
His number had gone up that day,
They might not heed his frightened eyes,
They shot him when the dawn was grey.
Blindfolded, when the dawn was grey,
He stood there in a place apart,

The shots rang out and down he fell,
An English bullet in his heart.
An English bullet in his heart!
But here's the irony of life, –
His mother thinks he fought and fell
A hero, foremost in the strife.
So she goes proudly; to the strife
Her best, her hero son she gave.
O well for her she does not know
He lies in a deserter's grave.

Winifred Letts

THE TWO MOTHERS

'Poor woman, weeping as they pass,
Yon brave recruits, the nation's pride,
You mourn some gallant boy, alas!
Like mine who lately fought and died?'

'Kind stranger, not for soldier son,
Of shame, not grief, my heart will break.
Three stalwarts have I, but not one
Doth risk his life for England's sake!'

Matilda Betham-Edwards

This Is No Case of Petty Right or Wrong

This is no case of petty right or wrong
That politicians or philosophers
Can judge. I hate not Germans, nor grow hot
With love of Englishmen, to please newspapers.
Beside my hate for one fat patriot
My hatred of the Kaiser is love true: –
A kind of god he is, banging a gong.
But I have not to choose between the two,
Or between justice and injustice. Dinned
With war and argument I read no more
Than in the storm smoking along the wind
Athwart the wood. Two witches' cauldrons roar.
From one the weather shall rise clear and gay;
Out of the other an England beautiful
And like her mother that died yesterday.
Little I know or care if, being dull,
I shall miss something that historians
Can rake out of the ashes when perchance
The phoenix broods serene above their ken.
But with the best and meanest Englishmen
I am one in crying, God save England, lest

We lose what never slaves and cattle blessed.
The ages made her that made us from dust:
She is all we know and live by, and we trust
She is good and must endure, loving her so:
And as we love ourselves we hate her foe.

Edward Thomas
26 December 1915

Break of Day in the Trenches

The darkness crumbles away –
It is the same old druid Time as ever.
Only a live thing leaps my hand –
A queer sardonic rat –
As I pull the parapet's poppy
To stick behind my ear.
Droll rat, they would shoot you if they knew
Your cosmopolitan sympathies.
Now you have touched this English hand
You will do the same to a German –
Soon, no doubt, if it be your pleasure
To cross the sleeping green between.
It seems you inwardly grin as you pass
Strong eyes, fine limbs, haughty athletes
Less chanced than you for life,
Bonds to the whims of murder,
Sprawled in the bowels of the earth,
The torn fields of France.

What do you see in our eyes
At the shrieking iron and flame
Hurled through still heavens?
What quaver – what heart aghast?

Isaac Rosenberg

REPORTED MISSING

My thought shall never be that you are dead:
Who laughed so lately in this quiet place.
The dear and deep-eyed humour of that face
Held something ever living, in Death's stead.
Scornful I hear the flat things they have said
And all their piteous platitudes of pain.
I laugh! I laugh! – For you will come again –
This heart would never beat if you were dead.
The world's adrowse in twilight hushfulness,
There's purple lilac in your little room,
And somewhere out beyond the evening gloom
Small boys are culling summer watercress.
Of these familiar things I have no dread
Being so very sure you are not dead.

Anna Gordon Keown

In Memoriam (Easter 1915)

The flowers left thick at nightfall in the wood
This Eastertide call into mind the men,
Now far from home, who, with their sweethearts,
  should
Have gathered them and will do never again.

Edward Thomas

ALL THE HILLS AND VALES ALONG

All the hills and vales along
Earth is bursting into song,
And the singers are the chaps
Who are going to die perhaps.
  O sing, marching men,
    Till the valleys ring again.
    Give your gladness to earth's keeping,
    So be glad, when you are sleeping.

Cast away regret and rue,
Think what you are marching to.
Little live, great pass.
Jesus Christ and Barabbas
Were found the same day.
This died, that went his way.
  So sing with joyful breath,
    For why, you are going to death.
    Teeming earth will surely store
    All the gladness that you pour.

Earth that never doubts nor fears,
Earth that knows of death, not tears,
Earth that bore with joyful ease
Hemlock for Socrates,
Earth that blossomed and was glad
'Neath the cross that Christ had,
Shall rejoice and blossom too
When the bullet reaches you.
  Wherefore, men marching
  On the road to death, sing!
  Pour your gladness on earth's head,
  So be merry, so be dead.

From the hills and valleys earth
Shouts back the sound of mirth,
Tramp of feet and lilt of song
Ringing all the road along.
All the music of their going,
Ringing swinging glad song-throwing,
Earth will echo still, when foot
Lies numb and voice mute.
   On, marching men, on
   To the gates of death with song.
   Sow your gladness for earth's reaping,
   So you may be glad, though sleeping.
   Strew your gladness on earth's bed,
   So be merry, so be dead.

Charles Sorley

INTO BATTLE

The naked earth is warm with Spring,
  And with green grass and bursting trees
Leans to the sun's gaze glorying,
  And quivers in the sunny breeze;

And life is colour and warmth and light,
  And a striving evermore for these;
And he is dead who will not fight;
  And who dies fighting has increase.

The fighting man shall from the sun
  Take warmth, and life from the glowing earth;
Speed with the light-foot winds to run,
  And with the trees to newer birth;
And find, when fighting shall be done,
  Great rest, and fullness after dearth.

All the bright company of Heaven
  Hold him in their high comradeship,
The Dog-Star, and the Sisters Seven,
  Orion's Belt and sworded hip.

The woodland trees that stand together,
  They stand to him each one a friend;
They gently speak in the windy weather;
  They guide to valley and ridge's end.

The kestrel hovering by day,
  And the little owls that call by night,
Bid him be swift and keen as they,
  As keen of ear, as swift of sight.

The blackbird sings to him, 'Brother, brother,
  If this be the last song you shall sing,
Sing well, for you may not sing another;
  Brother, sing.'

In dreary, doubtful waiting hours,
  Before the brazen frenzy starts,
The horses show him nobler powers;
  O patient eyes, courageous hearts!

And when the burning moment breaks,
  And all things else are out of mind,
And only joy of battle takes
  Him by the throat, and makes him blind,

Through joy and blindness he shall know,
    Not caring much to know, that still
Nor lead nor steel shall reach him, so
    That it be not the Destined Will.

The thundering line of battle stands,
    And in the air Death moans and sings;
But Day shall clasp him with strong hands,
    And Night shall fold him in soft wings.

Julian Grenfell
Flanders, April 1915

Rouen

Early morning over Rouen, hopeful, high,
   courageous morning,
And the laughter of adventure and the steepness of
   the stair,
And the dawn across the river, and the wind across
   the bridges,
And the empty littered station and the tired people
   there.

Can you recall those mornings and the hurry of
   awakening,
And the long-forgotten wonder if we should miss
   the way,
And the unfamiliar faces, and the coming of
   provisions,
And the freshness and the glory of the labour of
   the day?

Hot noontide over Rouen, and the sun upon the
  city,
Sun and dust unceasing, and the glare of cloudless
  skies,
And the voices of the Indians and the endless
  stream of soldiers,
And the clicking of the tatties, and the buzzing of
  the flies.

Can you recall those noontides and the reek of
  steam and coffee,
Heavy-laden noontides with the evening's peace to
  win,
And the little piles of Woodbines, and the sticky
  soda bottles,
And the crushes in the 'Parlour', and the letters
  coming in?

Quiet night-time over Rouen, and the station full
of soldiers,
All the youth and pride of England from the ends
of all the earth;
And the rifles piled together, and the creaking of
the sword-belts,
And the faces bent above them, and the gay, heart-
breaking mirth.

Can I forget the passage from the cool white-
bedded Aid Post
Past the long sun-blistered coaches of the khaki
Red Cross train
To the truck train full of wounded, and the
weariness and laughter,
And 'Good-bye, and thank you, Sister', and the
empty yards again?

Can you recall the parcels that we made them for
  the railroad,
Crammed and bulging parcels held together by
  their string,
And the voices of the sergeants who called the
  Drafts together,
And the agony and splendour when they stood to
  save the King?

Can you forget their passing, the cheering and the
  waving,
The little group of people at the doorway of the
  shed,
The sudden awful silence when the last train
  swung to darkness,
And the lonely desolation, and the mocking stars
  o'erhead?

Can you recall the midnights, and the footsteps of
    night watchers,
Men who came from darkness and went back to
    dark again,
And the shadows on the rail-lines and the
    all-inglorious labour,
And the promise of the daylight firing blue the
    window-pane?

Can you recall the passing through the kitchen
    door to morning,
Morning very still and solemn breaking slowly on
    the town,
And the early coastways engines that had met the
    ships at daybreak,
And the Drafts just out from England, and the day
    shift coming down?

Can you forget returning slowly, stumbling on the
    cobbles,
And the white-decked Red Cross barges dropping
    seawards for the tide,
And the search for English papers, and the blessed
    cool of water,
And the peace of half-closed shutters that shut out
    the world outside?

Can I forget the evenings and the sunsets on the
    island,
And the tall black ships at anchor far below our
    balcony,
And the distant call of bugles, and the white wine
    in the glasses,
And the long line of the street lamps, stretching
    Eastwards to the sea?

. . . When the world slips slow to darkness, when
   the office fire burns lower,
My heart goes out to Rouen, Rouen all the world
   away;
When other men remember I remember our
   Adventure
And the trains that go from Rouen at the ending
   of the day.

May Wedderburn Cannan
26 April–25 May l915

PERHAPS

(To R.A.L. Died of wounds in France,
23 December 1915)

Perhaps some day the sun will shine again,
   And I shall see that still the skies are blue,
And feel once more I do not live in vain,
   Although bereft of You.

Perhaps the golden meadows at my feet
   Will make the sunny hours of Spring seem gay,
And I shall find the white May blossoms sweet,
   Though You have passed away.

Perhaps the summer woods will shimmer bright,
   And crimson roses once again be fair,
And autumn harvest fields a rich delight,
   Although You are not there.

Perhaps some day I shall not shrink in pain
   To see the passing of the dying year,
And listen to the Christmas songs again,
   Although You cannot hear.

But, though kind Time may many joys renew,
    There is one greatest joy I shall not know
Again, because my heart for loss of You
    Was broken, long ago.

Vera Brittain
1st London General Hospital
February 1916

Before the Summer

When our men are marching lightly up and down,
When the pipes are playing through the little town,
I see a thin line swaying through wind and mud and
  rain
And the broken regiments come back to rest again.

Now the pipes are playing, now the drums are beat,
Now the strong battalions are marching up the
  street,
But the pipes will not be playing and the bayonets
  will not shine,
When the regiments I dream of come stumbling
  down the line.

Between the battered trenches their silent dead will
  lie
Quiet with grave eyes staring at the summer sky.
There is a mist upon them so that I cannot see
The faces of my friends that walk the little town
  with me.

Lest we see a worse thing than it is to die,
Live ourselves and see our friends cold beneath the
    sky,
God grant we too be lying there in wind and mud
    and rain
Before the broken regiments come stumbling back
    again.

E. A. Mackintosh
1916, before the Battle of the Somme

BEAUCOURT REVISITED

I wandered up to Beaucourt; I took the river track,
And saw the lines we lived in before the Boche went
  back;
But Peace was now in Pottage, the front was far
  ahead,
The front had journeyed Eastward, and only left the
  dead.

And I thought, How long we lay there, and watched
  across the wire,
While the guns roared round the valley, and set the
  skies afire!
But now there are homes in Hamel and tents in the
  Vale of Hell,
And a camp at Suicide Corner, where half a
  regiment fell.

The new troops follow after, and tread the land we
   won,
To them 'tis so much hillside re-wrested from the
   Hun;
We only walk with reverence this sullen mile of mud;
The shell-holes hold our history, and half of them our
   blood.

Here, at the head of Peche Street, 'twas death to show
   your face;
To me it seemed like magic to linger in the place;
For me how many spirits hung round the Kentish
   Caves,
But the new men see no spirits – they only see the
   graves.

I found the half-dug ditches we fashioned for the
   fight,
We lost a score of men there – young James was killed
   that night;
I saw the star-shells staring, I heard the bullets hail,
But the new troops pass unheeding – they never heard
   the tale.

I crossed the blood-red ribbon, that once was No
　　Man's Land,
I saw a misty daybreak and a creeping minute-hand;
And here the lads went over, and there was
　　Harmsworth shot,
And here was William lying – but the new men
　　know them not.

And I said, 'There is still the river, and still the stiff,
　　stark trees:
To treasure here our story, but there are only these';
But under the white wood crosses the dead men
　　answered low,
'The new men know not Beaucourt, but we are
　　here – we know.'

A. P. Herbert

The Last Laugh

'O Jesus Christ! I'm hit,' he said; and died.
Whether he vainly cursed, or prayed indeed,
The Bullets chirped—In vain! vain! vain!
Machine-guns chuckled,—Tut-tut! Tut-tut!
And the Big Gun guffawed.

Another sighed,—'O Mother, Mother! Dad!'
Then smiled, at nothing, childlike, being dead.
  And the lofty Shrapnel-cloud
  Leisurely gestured,—fool!
  And the falling splinters tittered.

'My Love!' one moaned. Love-languid seemed his
  mood,
Till, slowly lowered, his whole face kissed the mud.
  And the Bayonets' long teeth grinned;
  Rabbles of Shells hooted and groaned;
  And the Gas hissed.

Wilfred Owen

Soldiers

Brother,
I saw you on a muddy road
in France
pass by with your battalion,
rifle at the slope, full marching order,
arm swinging;
and I stood at ease,
folding my hands over my rifle,
with my battalion.
You passed me by, and our eyes met.
We had not seen each other since the days
we climbed the Devon hills together:
our eyes met, startled;
and, because the order was Silence,
we dared not speak.

O face of my friend,
alone distinct of all that company,
you went on, you went on,
into the darkness;
and I sit here at my table,
holding back my tears,
with my jaw set and my teeth clenched,
knowing I shall not be
even so near you as I saw you
in my dream.

F. S. Flint

The Owl

Downhill I came, hungry, and yet not starved;
Cold, yet had heat within me that was proof
Against the North wind; tired, yet so that rest
Had seemed the sweetest thing under a roof.

Then at the inn I had food, fire, and rest,
Knowing how hungry, cold, and tired was I.
All of the night was quite barred out except
An owl's cry, a most melancholy cry

Shaken out long and clear upon the hill,
No merry note, nor cause of merriment,
But one telling me plain what I escaped
And others could not, that night, as in I went.

And salted was my food, and my repose,
Salted and sobered, too, by the bird's voice
Speaking for all who lay under the stars,
Soldiers and poor, unable to rejoice.

Edward Thomas

To My Brother
(In memory of 1 July 1916)

Your battle-wounds are scars upon my heart,
   Received when in that grand and tragic 'show'
You played your part
   Two years ago,

And silver in the summer morning sun
   I see the symbol of your courage glow –
That Cross you won
   Two years ago.

Though now again you watch the shrapnel fly,
   And hear the guns that daily louder grow,
As in July
   Two years ago,

May you endure to lead the Last Advance
   And with your men pursue the flying foe
As once in France
   Two years ago.

Vera Brittain

Rendezvous

I have a rendezvous with Death
At some disputed barricade,
When Spring comes back with rustling shade
And apple-blossoms fill the air –
I have a rendezvous with Death
When Spring brings back blue days and fair.

It may be he shall take my hand
And lead me into his dark land
And close my eyes and quench my breath –
It may be I shall pass him still.
I have a rendezvous with Death
On some scarred slope of battered hill
When Spring comes round again this year
And the first meadow-flowers appear.

God knows 'twere better to be deep
Pillowed in silk and scented down,
Where love throbs out in blissful sleep,
Pulse nigh to pulse, and breath to breath,
Where hushed awakenings are dear . . .
But I've a rendezvous with Death
At midnight in some flaming town,
When Spring trips north again this year,
And I to my pledged word am true,
I shall not fail that rendezvous.

Alan Seeger
Written between January and February 1916

'SINCE THEY HAVE DIED'

Since they have died to give us gentleness,
And hearts kind with contentment and quiet mirth,
Let us who live give also happiness
And love, that's born of pity, to the earth.

For, I have thought, some day they may lie sleeping
Forgetting all the weariness and pain,
And smile to think their world is in our keeping,
And laughter come back to the earth again.

May Wedderburn Cannan
February 1916

LAMPLIGHT

We planned to shake the world together, you and I
Being young, and very wise;
Now in the light of the green shaded lamp
Almost I see your eyes
Light with the old gay laughter; you and I
Dreamed greatly of an Empire in those days,
Setting our feet upon laborious ways,
And all you asked of fame
Was crossed swords in the Army List,
My Dear, against your name.

We planned a great Empire together, you and I,
Bound only by the sea;
Now in the quiet of a chill Winter's night
Your voice comes hushed to me
Full of forgotten memories: you and I
Dreamed great dreams of our future in those days,
Setting our feet on undiscovered ways,
And all I asked of fame
A scarlet cross on my breast, my Dear,
For the swords by your name.

We shall never shake the world together, you and I,
For you gave your life away;
And I think my heart was broken by the war,
Since on a summer day
You took the road we never spoke of: you and I
Dreamed greatly of an Empire in those days;
You set your feet upon the Western ways
And have no need of fame –
There's a scarlet cross on my breast, my Dear,
And a torn cross with your name.

May Wedderburn Cannan
December 1916

Despair

Half of me died at Bapaume,
    And the rest of me is a log:
For my soul was in the other half;
    And the half that is here is a clog
On the one who would always be doing
    In days never to come again.
Carry me into the darkness, sir,
    And put me out of my pain.

The best of me died at Bapaume
    When the world went up in fire,
And the soul that was mine deserted
    And left me, a thing in the mire,
With a madden'd and dim remembrance
    Of a time when my life was whole.
Carry me into the darkness, sir,
    And let me find my soul.

If half of you went at Bapaume,
   And with it your soul went too,
That soul has laid as a sacrifice
   The half that was torn from you.
At the feet of the One who Himself has given,
   Laid all that a man can give;
And then will return to the other half
   And show it how to live.

Olive E. Lindsay

Lights Out

I have come to the borders of sleep,
The unfathomable deep
Forest where all must lose
Their way, however straight,
Or winding, soon or late;
They cannot choose.

Many a road and track
That, since the dawn's first crack,
Up to the forest brink,
Deceived the travellers,
Suddenly now blurs,
And in they sink.

Here love ends,
Despair, ambition ends;
All pleasure and all trouble,
Although most sweet or bitter,
Here ends in sleep that is sweeter
Than tasks most noble.

There is not any book
Or face of dearest look
That I would not turn from now
To go into the unknown
I must enter, and leave, alone.
I know not how.

The tall forest towers;
Its cloudy foliage lowers
Ahead, shelf above shelf;
Its silence I hear and obey
That I may lose my way
And myself.

Edward Thomas
November 1916

Out in the Dark

Out in the dark over the snow
The fallow fawns invisible go
With the fallow doe;
And the winds blow
Fast as the stars are slow.

Stealthily the dark haunts round
And, when the lamp goes, without sound
At a swifter bound
Than the swiftest hound,
Arrives, and all else is drowned;

And star and I and wind and deer,
Are in the dark together, – near,
Yet far, – and fear
Drums on my ear
In that sage company drear.

How weak and little is the light,
All the universe of sight,
Love and delight,
Before the might,
If you love it not, of night.

Edward Thomas
24 December 1916

THE TRUMPET

Rise up, rise up,
And, as the trumpet blowing
Chases the dreams of men,
As the dawn glowing
The stars that left unlit
The land and water,
Rise up and scatter
The dew that covers
The print of last night's lovers –
Scatter it, scatter it!

While you are listening
To the clear horn,
Forget, men, everything
On this earth new-born,
Except that it is lovelier
Than any mysteries.
Open your eyes to the air
That has washed the eyes of the stars
Through all the dewy night:
Up with the light,
To the old wars;
Arise, arise!

Edward Thomas
26–28 May 1916

As the Team's Head Brass

As the team's head brass flashed out on the turn
The lovers disappeared into the wood.
I sat among the boughs of the fallen elm
That strewed an angle of the fallow, and
Watched the plough narrowing a yellow square
Of charlock. Every time the horses turned
Instead of treading me down, the ploughman leaned
Upon the handles to say or ask a word,
About the weather, next about the war.
Scraping the share he faced towards the wood,
And screwed along the furrow till the brass flashed
Once more.
     The blizzard felled the elm whose crest
I sat in, by a woodpecker's round hole,
The ploughman said. 'When will they take it away?'
'When the war's over.' So the talk began—
One minute and an interval of ten,
A minute more and the same interval.
'Have you been out?' 'No.' 'And don't want to,
 perhaps?'

'If I could only come back again, I should.
I could spare an arm. I shouldn't want to lose
A leg. If I should lose my head, why, so,
I should want nothing more. . . . Have many gone
From here?' 'Yes.' 'Many lost?' 'Yes, a good few.
Only two teams work on the farm this year.
One of my mates is dead. The second day
In France they killed him. It was back in March,
The very night of the blizzard, too. Now if
He had stayed here we should have moved the tree.'
'And I should not have sat here. Everything
Would have been different. For it would have been
Another world.' 'Ay, and a better, though
If we could see all all might seem good.' Then
The lovers came out of the wood again:
The horses started and for the last time
I watched the clods crumble and topple over
After the ploughshare and the stumbling team.

Edward Thomas

ANTHEM FOR DOOMED YOUTH

What passing-bells for these who die as cattle?
　　Only the monstrous anger of the guns.
　　Only the stuttering rifles' rapid rattle
Can patter out their hasty orisons.
No mockeries now for them, no prayers nor bells;
　　Nor any voice of mourning save the choirs, –
The shrill demented choirs of wailing shells;
　　And bugles calling for them from sad shires.

What candles may be held to speed them all?
　　Not in the hands of boys but in their eyes
Shall shine the holy glimmers of goodbyes.
　　The pallor of girls' brows shall be their pall;
Their flowers the tenderness of patient minds,
　　And each slow dusk a drawing-down of blinds.

Wilfred Owen

Spring 1917

It is spring.
The buds break softly, silently.
This evening
The air is pink with the low sun,
And birds sing.

Do we believe
Men are now killing, dying—
This evening,
While the sky is pink with the low sun,
And birds sing?

No . . .
So they go on killing, dying,
This evening,
And through summer, autumn, winter,
And through spring.

Beatrice Mayor

SEARCHLIGHT

There has been no sound of guns,
No roar of exploding bombs;
But the darkness has an edge
That grits the nerves of the sleeper.

He awakens;
Nothing disturbs the stillness,
Save perhaps the light, slow flap,
Once only, of the curtain
Dim in the darkness.

Yet there is something else
That drags him from his bed;
And he stands in the darkness
With his feet cold against the floor
And the cold air round his ankles.
He does not know why,
But he goes to the window and sees
A beam of light, miles high,
Dividing the night into two before him,
Still, stark and throbbing.

The houses and gardens beneath
Lie under the snow
Quiet and tinged with purple.

There has been no sound of guns,
No roar of exploding bombs;
Only that watchfulness hidden among the snow-
   covered houses,
And that great beam thrusting back into heaven
The light taken from it.

F. S. Flint

To His Love

He's gone, and all our plans
  Are useless indeed.
We'll walk no more on Cotswold
  Where the sheep feed
 Quietly and take no heed.

His body that was so quick
  Is not as you
Knew it, on Severn river
  Under the blue
  Driving our small boat through.

You would not know him now . . .
  But still he died
Nobly, so cover him over
  With violets of pride
  Purple from Severn side.

Cover him, cover him soon!
  And with thick-set
Masses of memoried flowers—
  Hide that red wet
  Thing I must somehow forget.

Ivor Gurney

GREATER LOVE

Red lips are not so red
　　As the stained stones kissed by the English dead.
Kindness of wooed and wooer
Seems shame to their love pure.
O Love, your eyes lose lure
　　When I behold eyes blinded in my stead!

Your slender attitude
　　Trembles not exquisite like limbs knife-skewed,
Rolling and rolling there
Where God seems not to care;
Till the fierce Love they bear
　　Cramps them in death's extreme decrepitude.

Your voice sings not so soft,—
　　Though even as wind murmuring through
　　　　　　　　　　　　　　raftered loft,—
Your dear voice is not dear,
Gentle, and evening clear,
As theirs whom none now hear
　　Now earth has stopped their piteous mouths that
　　　　　　　　　　　　　　coughed.

Heart, you were never hot,
    Nor large, nor full like hearts made great with shot;
And though your hand be pale,
Paler are all which trail
Your cross through flame and hail:
    Weep, you may weep, for you may touch them not.

Wilfred Owen

Base Details

If I were fierce, and bald, and short of breath,
I'd live with scarlet Majors at the Base,
And speed glum heroes up the line to death.
You'd see me with my puffy, petulant face,
Guzzling and gulping in the best hotel,
Reading the Roll of Honour. 'Poor young chap,'
I'd say – 'I used to know his father well;
Yes, we've lost heavily in this last scrap.'
And when the war is done and youth stone dead,
I'd toddle safely home and die – in bed.

Siegfried Sassoon
4 March 1917

Dulce Et Decorum Est

Bent double, like old beggars under sacks,
Knock-kneed, coughing like hags, we cursed
   through sludge,
Till on the haunting flares we turned our backs
And towards our distant rest began to trudge.
Men marched asleep. Many had lost their boots
But limped on, blood-shod. All went lame; all blind;
Drunk with fatigue; deaf even to the hoots
Of disappointed shells that dropped behind.

GAS! Gas! Quick, boys!— An ecstasy of fumbling,
Fitting the clumsy helmets just in time;
But someone still was yelling out and stumbling
And floundering like a man in fire or lime.—
Dim, through the misty panes and thick green light
As under a green sea, I saw him drowning.

In all my dreams, before my helpless sight,
He plunges at me, guttering, choking, drowning.

If in some smothering dreams you too could pace
Behind the wagon that we flung him in,
And watch the white eyes writhing in his face,
His hanging face, like a devil's sick of sin;
If you could hear, at every jolt, the blood
Come gargling from the froth-corrupted lungs,
Obscene as cancer, bitter as the cud
Of vile, incurable sores on innocent tongues,—
My friend, you would not tell with such high zest
To children ardent for some desperate glory,
The old Lie: Dulce et decorum est
Pro patria mori.

Wilfred Owen

THE SILENT ONE

Who died on the wires, and hung there, one of
  two –
Who for his hours of life had chattered through
Infinite lovely chatter of Bucks accent:
Yet faced unbroken wires; stepped over, and went
A noble fool, faithful to his stripes – and ended.
But I weak, hungry, and willing only for the chance
Of line – to fight in the line, lay down under
  unbroken
Wires, and saw the flashes and kept unshaken,
Till the politest voice – a finicking accent, said:
'Do you think you might crawl through, there:
  there's a hole'
Darkness, shot at: I smiled, as politely replied –
'I'm afraid not, Sir.' There was no hole no way to be
  seen
Nothing but chance of death, after tearing of
  clothes
Kept flat, and watched the darkness, hearing bullets
  whizzing –
And thought of music – and swore deep heart's
  deep oaths

(Polite to God) and retreated and came on again,
Again retreated – and a second time faced the
  screen.

Ivor Gurney

In the Church of St Ouen

Time makes me be a soldier. But I know
That had I lived six hundred years ago
I might have tried to build within my heart
A church like this, where I could dwell apart
With chanting peace. My spirit longs for prayer;
And, lost to God, I seek him everywhere.

Here, where the windows burn and bloom like
   flowers,
And sunlight falls and fades with tranquil hours,
I could be half a saint, for like a rose
In heart-shaped stone the glory of Heaven glows.
But where I stand, desiring yet to stay,
Hearing rich music at the close of day,
The Spring Offensive (Easter is its date)
Calls me. And that's the music I await.

Siegfried Sassoon
At Rouen, 4 March 1917

THE WIND ON THE DOWNS

I like to think of you as brown and tall,
As strong and living as you used to be,
In khaki tunic, Sam Brown belt and all,
And standing there and laughing down at me,
Because they tell me, dear, that you are dead.
Because I can no longer see your face.
You have not died, it is not true, instead
You seek adventure in some other place.
That you are round about me, I believe;
I hear you laughing as you used to do,
Yet loving all the things I think of you;
And knowing you are happy, should I grieve?
You follow and are watchful where I go;
How should you leave me, having loved me so?

We walked along the tow-path, you and I,
Beside the sluggish-moving, still canal;
It seemed impossible that you should die;
I think of you the same and always shall.
We thought of many things and spoke of few,
And life lay all uncertainly before,
And now I walk alone and think of you,
And wonder what new kingdoms you explore.
Over the railway line, across the grass,
While up above the golden wings are spread,
Flying, ever flying overhead,
Here still I see your khaki figure pass,
And when I leave the meadow, almost wait
That you should open first the wooden gate.

Marian Allen

Returning, We Hear the Larks

Sombre the night is.
And though we have our lives, we know
What sinister threat lurks there.

Dragging these anguished limbs, we only know
This poison-blasted track opens on our camp—
On a little safe sleep.

But hark! joy—joy—strange joy.
Lo! heights of night ringing with unseen larks.
Music showering our upturned list'ning faces.

Death could drop from the dark
As easily as song—
But song only dropped,
Like a blind man's dreams on the sand
By dangerous tides,
Like a girl's dark hair for she dreams no ruin lies
    there,
Or her kisses where a serpent hides.

Isaac Rosenberg

EASTER MONDAY

(In memoriam E.T.)

In the last letter that I had from France
You thanked me for the silver Easter egg
Which I had hidden in the box of apples
You liked to munch beyond all other fruit.
You found the egg the Monday before Easter,
And said, 'I will praise Easter Monday now –
It was such a lovely morning'. Then you spoke
Of the coming battle and said, 'This is the eve.
Good-bye. And may I have a letter soon.'

That Easter Monday was a day for praise,
It was such a lovely morning. In our garden
We sowed our earliest seeds, and in the orchard
The apple-bud was ripe. It was the eve.
There are three letters that you will not get.

Eleanor Farjeon
9 April 1917

Vlamertinghe: Passing the Château, July, 1917

'And all her silken flanks with garlands drest' –
But we are coming to the sacrifice.
Must those have flowers who are not yet gone West?
May those have flowers who live with death and lice?
This must be the floweriest place
That earth allows; the queenly face
Of the proud mansion borrows grace for grace
Spite of those brute guns lowing at the skies.

Bold great daisies' golden lights,
Bubbling roses' pinks and whites –
Such a gay carpet! poppies by the million;
Such damask! such vermilion!
But if you ask me, mate, the choice of colour
Is scarcely right; this red should have been duller.

Edmund Blunden

Troopship: Mid-Atlantic

Dark waters into crystalline brilliance break
About the keel as, through the moonless night,
The dark ship moves in its own moving lake
Of phosphorescent cold moon-coloured light;
And to the clear horizon all around
Drift pools of fiery beryl flashing bright,
As though unquenchably burning cold and white
A million moons in the night of waters drowned.

And staring at the magic with eyes adream
That never till now have looked upon the sea,
Boys from the Middle West lounge listlessly
In the unlanthorned darkness, boys who go,
Beckoned by some unchallengeable dream,
To unknown lands to fight an unknown foe.

W. W. Gibson
On the S.S. Baltic, *July 1917*

MENTAL CASES

Who are these? Why sit they here in twilight?
Wherefore rock they, purgatorial shadows,
Drooping tongues from jaws that slob their relish,
Baring teeth that leer like skulls' tongues wicked?
Stroke on stroke of pain, — but what slow panic,
Gouged these chasms round their fretted sockets?
Ever from their hair and through their hand palms
Misery swelters. Surely we have perished
Sleeping, and walk hell; but who these hellish?

— These are men whose minds the Dead have
    ravished.
Memory fingers in their hair of murders,
Multitudinous murders they once witnessed.
Wading sloughs of flesh these helpless wander,
Treading blood from lungs that had loved laughter.
Always they must see these things and hear them,
Batter of guns and shatter of flying muscles,
Carnage incomparable and human squander
Rucked too thick for these men's extrication.

Therefore still their eyeballs shrink tormented
Back into their brains, because on their sense
Sunlight seems a bloodsmear; night comes blood-
    black;
Dawn breaks open like a wound that bleeds afresh
— Thus their heads wear this hilarious, hideous,
Awful falseness of set-smiling corpses.
— Thus their hands are plucking at each other;
Picking at the rope-knouts of their scourging;
Snatching after us who smote them, brother,
Pawing us who dealt them war and madness.

Wilfred Owen

Convalescence

From out the dragging vastness of the sea,
   Wave-fettered, bound in sinuous seaweed strands,
   He toils toward the rounding beach, and stands
One moment, white and dripping, silently,
Cut like a cameo in lazuli,
   Then falls, betrayed by shifting shells, and lands
   Prone in the jeering water, and his hands
Clutch for support where no support can be.
   So up, and down, and forward, inch by inch,
He gains upon the shore, where poppies glow
And sandflies dance their little lives away.
   The sucking waves retard, and tighter clinch
The weeds about him, but the land-winds blow,
And in the sky there blooms the sun of May.

Amy Lowell

The Convalescent

We've billards, bowls an' tennis courts, we've teas
    an' motor-rides;
We've concerts nearly every night, an' 'eaps o'
    things besides;
We've all the best of everything as much as we can
    eat —
But my 'eart — my 'eart's at 'ome in 'Enry Street.

I'm askin' Sister every day when I'll be fit to go;
'We must 'ave used you bad' (she says) 'you want
    to leave us so';
I says, 'I beg your pardon, Nurse, the place is 'ard
    to beat,
But my 'eart — my 'eart's at 'ome in 'Enry Street.'

The sheffoneer we saved to buy, the clock upon
    the wall,
The pictures an' the almanac, the china dogs an'
    all,
I've thought about it many a time, my little 'ome
    complete,
When in Flanders, far away from 'Enry Street.

It's 'elped me through the toughest times – an'
   some was middlin' tough –
The 'ardest march was not so 'ard, the roughest not
   so rough;
It's 'elped me keep my pecker up in victory an'
   defeat,
Just to think about my 'ome in 'Enry Street.

There's several things I'd like to 'ave which 'ere I
   never see,
I'd like some chipped potatoes an' a kipper to my
   tea;
But most of all I'd like to feel the stones beneath
   my feet
Of the road that takes me 'ome to 'Enry Street.

They'll 'ave a little flag 'ung out – they'll 'ave the
   parlour gay
With crinkled paper all about, the same as
   Christmas Day,
An' out of all the neighbours' doors the 'eads 'll
   pop to greet
Me comin' wounded 'ome to 'Enry Street.

My missis – well, she'll cry a bit, an' laugh a bit
  between;
My kids 'll climb upon my knees – there's one I've
  never seen;
An' of all the days which I 'ave known there won't
  be one so sweet
As the one when I go 'ome to 'Enry Street.

Cicily Fox Smith

SING A SONG OF WAR-TIME

Sing a song of War-time,
Soldiers marching by,
Crowds of people standing,
Waving them 'Good-bye'.
When the crowds are over,
Home we go to tea,
Bread and margarine to eat,
War economy!

If I ask for cake, or
Jam of any sort,
Nurse says, 'What! in War-time?
Archie, cert'nly not!'
Life's not very funny
Now, for little boys,
Haven't any money,
Can't buy any toys.

Mummie does the house-work,
Can't get any maid,
Gone to make munitions,
'Cause they're better paid,
Nurse is always busy,
Never time to play,
Sewing shirts for soldiers,
Nearly ev'ry day.

Ev'ry body's doing
Something for the War,
Girls are doing things
They've never done before,
Go as 'bus conductors,
Drive a car or van,
All the world is topsy-turvy
Since the War began.

Nina Macdonald

MUNITION WAGES

Earning high wages? Yus,
    Five quid a week.
A woman, too, mind you,
    I calls it dim sweet.

Ye'are asking some questions –
    But bless yer, here goes:
I spends the whole racket
    On good times and clothes.

Me saving? Elijah!
    Yer do think I'm mad.
I'm acting the lady,
    But – I ain't living bad.

I'm having life's good times.
    See 'ere, it's like this:
The 'oof come o' danger,
    A touch-and-go bizz.

We're all here today, mate,
    Tomorrow – perhaps dead,
If Fate tumbles on us
    And blows up our shed.

Afraid! Are yer kidding?
   With money to spend!
Years back I wore tatters,
   Now – silk stockings, mi friend!

I've bracelets and jewellery,
   Rings envied by friends;
A sergeant to swank with,
   And something to lend.

I drive out in taxis,
   Do theatres in style.
And this is mi verdict –
   It is jolly worth while.

Worth while, for tomorrow
   If I'm blown to the sky,
I'll have repaid mi wages
   In death – and pass by.

Madeline Ida Bedford

WAR GIRLS

There's the girl who clips your ticket for the train,
  And the girl who speeds the lift from floor to floor,
There's the girl who does a milk-round in the rain,
  And the girl who calls for orders at your door.
      Strong, sensible, and fit,
      They're out to show their grit,
    And tackle jobs with energy and knack.
      No longer caged and penned up,
      They're going to keep their end up
    Till the khaki soldier boys come marching back.

There's the motor girl who drives a heavy van,
  There's the butcher girl who brings your joint of
                                                    meat,
There's the girl who cries 'All fares, please!' like a
                                                    man,
  And the girl who whistles taxis up the street.

Beneath each uniform
Beats a heart that's soft and warm,
Though of canny mother-wit they show no lack;
But a solemn statement this is,
They've no time for love and kisses
Till the khaki soldier boys come marching back.

Jessie Pope

MANY SISTERS TO MANY BROTHERS

When we fought campaigns (in the long
                                    Christmas rains)
  With soldiers spread in troops on the floor,
I shot as straight as you, my losses were as few,
  My victories as many, or more.
And when in naval battle, amid cannon's rattle,
  Fleet met fleet in the bath,
My cruisers were as trim, my battleships as grim,
  My submarines cut as swift a path.
Or, when it rained too long, and the strength of
                                    the strong
  Surged up and broke a way with blows,
I was as fit and keen, my fists hit as clean,
  Your black eye matched my bleeding nose.
Was there a scrap or ploy in which you, the boy,
  Could better me? You could not climb higher,
Ride straighter, run as quick (and to smoke made
                                    you sick)
  . . . But I sit here and you're under fire.

Oh, it's you that have the luck, out there in blood
and muck:
    You were born beneath a kindly star;
All we dreamt, I and you, you can really go and do,
    And I can't, the way things are.
In a trench you are sitting, while I am knitting
    A hopeless sock that never gets done.
Well, here's luck, my dear; – and you've got it, no
fear;
    But for me . . . a war is poor fun.

Rose Macaulay

PICNIC

We lay and ate sweet hurt-berries
   In the bracken of Hurt Wood.
Like a quire of singers singing low
   The dark pines stood.

Behind us climbed the Surrey hills,
   Wild, wild in greenery;
At our feet the downs of Sussex broke
   To an unseen sea.

And life was bound in a still ring,
   Drowsy, and quiet, and sweet . . .
When heavily up the south-east wind
   The great guns beat.

We did not wince, we did not weep,
   We did not curse or pray;
We drowsily heard, and someone said,
   'They sound clear today'.

We did not shake with pity and pain,
  Or sicken and blanch white.
We said, 'If the wind's from over there
  There'll be rain tonight'.

Once pity we knew, and rage we knew,
  And pain we knew, too well,
As we stared and peered dizzily
  Through the gates of hell.

But now hell's gates are an old tale;
  Remote the anguish seems;
The guns are muffled and far away,
  Dreams within dreams.

And far and far are Flanders mud,
  And the pain of Picardy;
And the blood that runs there runs beyond
  The wide waste sea.

We are shut about by guarding walls:
  (We have built them lest we run
Mad from dreaming of naked fear
  And of black things done).

We are ringed all round by guarding walls,
  So high, they shut the view.
Not all the guns that shatter the world
  Can quite break through.

Oh, guns of France, oh, guns of France,
  Be still, you crash in vain. . . .
Heavily up the south wind throb
  Dull dreams of pain, . . .

Be still, be still, south wind, lest your
  Blowing should bring the rain. . . .
We'll lie very quiet on Hurt Hill,
  And sleep once again.

Oh, we'll lie quite still, nor listen nor look,
  While the earth's bounds reel and shake,
Lest, battered too long, our walls and we
  Should break . . . should break. . . .

Rose Macaulay
July 1917

At the Movies

They swing across the screen in brave array,
  Long British columns grinding the dark grass.
Twelve months ago they marched into the grey
  Of battle; yet again behold them pass!

One lifts his dusty cap; his hair is bright;
  I meet his eyes, eager and young and bold.
The picture quivers into ghostly white;
  Then I remember, and my heart grows cold!

Florence Ripley Mastin
January 1916

AIR-RAID

Night shatters in mid-heaven – the bark of guns,
The roar of planes, the crash of bombs, and all
The unshackled skyey pandemonium stuns
The senses to indifference, when a fall
Of masonry nearby startles awake,
Tingling, wide-eyed, prick-eared, with bristling hair,
Each sense within the body, crouched aware
Like some sore-hunted creature in the brake.

Yet side by side we lie in the little room,
Just touching hands, with eyes and ears that strain
Keenly, yet dream-bewildered, through tense gloom,
Listening, in helpless stupor of insane
Drugged nightmare panic fantastically wild,
To the quiet breathing of our little child.

W. W. Gibson

To Tony (AGED 3)
(In memory T.P.C.W.)

Gemmed with white daisies was the great green
world
Your restless feet have pressed this long day through –
Come now and let me whisper to your dreams
A little song grown from my love for you.

There was a man once loved green fields like you,
He drew his knowledge from the wild birds' songs;
And he had praise for every beauteous thing,
And he had pity for all piteous wrongs. . . .

A lover of earth's forests – of her hills,
And brother to her sunlight – to her rain –
Man, with a boy's fresh wonder. He was great
With greatness all too simple to explain.

He was a dreamer and a poet, and brave
To face and hold what he alone found true.
He was a comrade of the old – a friend
To every little laughing child like you.

And when across the peaceful English land,
Unhurt by war, the light is growing dim,
   And you remember by your shadowed bed
All those – the brave – you must remember him.

   And know it was for you who bear his name
And such as you that all his joy he gave –
   His love of quiet fields, his youth, his life,
To win that heritage of peace you have.

Marjorie Wilson

STRANGE MEETING

It seemed that out of battle I escaped
Down some profound dull tunnel, long since
   scooped
Through granites which titanic wars had groined.
Yet also there encumbered sleepers groaned,
Too fast in thought or death to be bestirred.
Then, as I probed them, one sprang up, and stared
With piteous recognition in fixed eyes,
Lifting distressful hands as if to bless.
And by his smile, I knew that sullen hall,
By his dead smile I knew we stood in Hell.
With a thousand pains that vision's face was grained;
Yet no blood reached there from the upper ground,
And no guns thumped, or down the flues made
   moan.
'Strange, friend,' I said, 'here is no cause to mourn.'
'None,' said the other, 'save the undone years,
The hopelessness. Whatever hope is yours,
Was my life also; I went hunting wild
After the wildest beauty in the world,
Which lies not calm in eyes, or braided hair,

But mocks the steady running of the hour,
And if it grieves, grieves richlier than here.
For by my glee might many men have laughed,
And of my weeping something had been left,
Which must die now. I mean the truth untold,
The pity of war, the pity war distilled.
Now men will go content with what we spoiled.
Or, discontent, boil bloody, and be spilled.
They will be swift with swiftness of the tigress,
None will break ranks, though nations trek from
  progress.
Courage was mine, and I had mystery;
Wisdom was mine, and I had mastery;
To miss the march of this retreating world
Into vain citadels that are not walled.
Then, when much blood had clogged their chariot-
  wheels
I would go up and wash them from sweet wells,
Even with truths that lie too deep for taint.
I would have poured my spirit without stint
But not through wounds; not on the cess of war.
Foreheads of men have bled where no wounds were.

I am the enemy you killed, my friend.
I knew you in this dark; for so you frowned
Yesterday through me as you jabbed and killed.
I parried; but my hands were loath and cold.
Let us sleep now . . .'

Wilfred Owen

ASSAULT

Gas!
faces turned,
eyes scanned the sky,
hands feverishly ripped open canisters,
and masks were soon covering faces.
A man choked
as the white cloud,
swirling round him like fog, caught him
unawares.
Then his body flopped over.
Shells floated across
as if suspended by hidden strings,
and then, tired,
they sank earthwards.

A command!
I fixed my bayonet,
scrambled over the open trench
and struggled through
the thick pasty mud.

It was quiet
as we walked
except for the sucking,
groaning, squelching sound
which came from the wet earth
as it tried
to creep into our stockings.
The wind cut me.

Over the wall!
Then a whistle.
'Good luck, mates.'
Mind that hole. Through the wire.
Over the top.
And kill.
'God. This is fun!'

Erno Muller

THE DUG-OUT

Why do you lie with your legs ungainly huddled,
And one arm bent across your sullen, cold,
Exhausted face? It hurts my heart to watch you,
Deep-shadow'd from the candle's guttering gold;
And you wonder why I shake you by the shoulder;
Drowsy, you mumble and sigh and turn your head . . .
You are too young to fall asleep for ever;
And when you sleep you remind me of the dead.

Siegfried Sassoon

Insensibility

I

Happy are men who yet before they are killed
Can let their veins run cold.
Whom no compassion fleers
Or makes their feet
Sore on the alleys cobbled with their brothers.
The front line withers,
But they are troops who fade, not flowers
For poets' tearful fooling:
Men, gaps for filling
Losses who might have fought
Longer; but no one bothers.

II

And some cease feeling
Even themselves or for themselves.
Dullness best solves
The tease and doubt of shelling,
And Chance's strange arithmetic
Comes simpler than the reckoning of their shilling.
They keep no check on Armies' decimation.

III

Happy are these who lose imagination:
They have enough to carry with ammunition.
Their spirit drags no pack.
Their old wounds save with cold can not more ache.
Having seen all things red,
Their eyes are rid
Of the hurt of the colour of blood for ever.
And terror's first constriction over,
Their hearts remain small drawn.
Their senses in some scorching cautery of battle
Now long since ironed,
Can laugh among the dying, unconcerned.

IV

Happy the soldier home, with not a notion
How somewhere, every dawn, some men attack,
And many sighs are drained.
Happy the lad whose mind was never trained:
His days are worth forgetting more than not.
He sings along the march
Which we march taciturn, because of dusk,
The long, forlorn, relentless trend
From larger day to huger night.

V

We wise, who with a thought besmirch
Blood over all our soul,
How should we see our task
But through his blunt and lashless eyes?
Alive, he is not vital overmuch;
Dying, not mortal overmuch;
Nor sad, nor proud,
Nor curious at all.
He cannot tell
Old men's placidity from his.

VI

But cursed are dullards whom no cannon stuns,
That they should be as stones.
Wretched are they, and mean
With paucity that never was simplicity.
By choice they made themselves immune
To pity and whatever mourns in man
Before the last sea and the hapless stars;
Whatever mourns when many leave these shores;
Whatever shares
The eternal reciprocity of tears.

Wilfred Owen

Exposure

Our brains ache, in the merciless iced east winds that
  knive us . . .
Wearied we keep awake because the night is silent . . .
Low, drooping flares confuse our memory of the
  salient . . .
Worried by silence, sentries whisper, curious, nervous,
But nothing happens.

Watching, we hear the mad gusts tugging on the
  wire,
Like twitching agonies of men among its brambles.
Northward, incessantly, the flickering gunnery
  rumbles,
Far off, like a dull rumour of some other war.
What are we doing here?

The poignant misery of dawn begins to grow . . .
We only know war lasts, rain soaks, and clouds sag
  stormy.
Dawn massing in the east her melancholy army
Attacks once more in ranks on shivering ranks of gray,
But nothing happens.

Sudden successive flights of bullets streak the silence.
Less deathly than the air that shudders black with
    snow,
With sidelong flowing flakes that flock, pause, and
    renew;
We watch them wandering up and down the wind's
    nonchalance,
But nothing happens.

Pale flakes with fingering stealth come feeling for our
    faces –
We cringe in holes, back on forgotten dreams, and
    stare, snow-dazed,
Deep into grassier ditches. So we drowse, sun-dozed,
Littered with blossoms trickling where the blackbird
    fusses.
Is it that we are dying?

Slowly our ghosts drag home: glimpsing the sunk
   fires, glozed
With crusted dark-red jewels; crickets jingle there;
For hours the innocent mice rejoice: the house is
   theirs;
Shutters and doors, all closed: on us the doors are
   closed, –
We turn back to our dying.

Since we believe not otherwise can kind fires burn;
Nor ever suns smile true on child, or field, or fruit.
For God's invincible spring our love is made afraid;
Therefore, not loath, we lie out here; therefore were
   born,
For love of God seems dying.

Tonight, this frost will fasten on this mud and us,
Shrivelling many hands, puckering foreheads crisp.
The burying-party, picks and shovels in their shaking
   grasp,
Pause over half-known faces. All their eyes are ice,
But nothing happens.

Wilfred Owen
Completed in September 1918

Rain

Rain, midnight rain, nothing but the wild rain
On this bleak hut, and solitude, and me
Remembering again that I shall die
And neither hear the rain nor give it thanks
For washing me cleaner than I have been
Since I was born into this solitude.
Blessed are the dead that the rain rains upon:
But here I pray that none whom once I loved
Is dying tonight or lying still awake
Solitary, listening to the rain,
Either in pain or thus in sympathy
Helpless among the living and the dead,
Like a cold water among broken reeds,
Myriads of broken reeds all still and stiff,
Like me who have no love which this wild rain
Has not dissolved except the love of death,
If love it be towards what is perfect and
Cannot, the tempest tells me, disappoint.

Edward Thomas

Two Voices

'There's something in the air,' he said
  In the farm parlour cool and bare;
Plain words, which in his hearers bred
  A tumult, yet in silence there
All waited; wryly gay, he left the phrase,
Ordered the march, and bade us go our ways.

'We're going South, man'; as he spoke
  The howitzer with huge ping-bang
Racked the light hut; as thus he broke
  The death-news, bright the skylarks sang;
He took his riding-crop and humming went
Among the apple-trees all bloom and scent.

Now far withdraws the roaring night
  Which wrecked our flower after the first
Of those two voices; misty light
  Shrouds Thiepval Wood and all its worst;
But still 'There's something in the air' I hear,
And still 'We're going South, man' deadly near.

Edmund Blunden

FUTILITY

Move him into the sun –
Gently its touch awoke him once,
At home, whispering of fields unsown.
Always it woke him, even in France,
Until this morning and this snow.
If anything might rouse him now
The kind old sun will know.

Think how it wakes the seeds –
Woke, once, the clays of a cold star.
Are limbs, so dear achieved, are sides
Full-nerved – still warm – too hard to stir?
Was it for this the clay grew tall?
O what made fatuous sunbeams toil
To break earth's sleep at all?

Wilfred Owen
May 1918

Magpies in Picardy

The magpies in Picardy
Are more than I can tell.
They flicker down the dusty roads
And cast a magic spell
On the men who march through Picardy,
Through Picardy to hell.

(The blackbird flies with panic,
The swallow goes with light,
The finches move like ladies,
The owl floats by at night;
But the great and flashing magpie
He flies as artists might.)

A magpie in Picardy
Told me secret things –
Of the music in white feathers,
And the sunlight that sings
And dances in deep shadows –
He told me with his wings.

(The hawk is cruel and rigid,
He watches from a height;
The rook is slow and sombre,
The robin loves to fight;
But the great and flashing magpie
He flies as lovers might.)

He told me that in Picardy,
An age ago or more,
While all his fathers still were eggs,
These dusty highways bore
Brown, singing soldiers marching out
Through Picardy to war.

He said that still through chaos
Works on the ancient plan,
And two things have altered not
Since first the world began –
The beauty of the wild green earth
And the bravery of man.

(For the sparrow flies unthinking
And quarrels in his flight;
The heron trails his legs behind,
The lark goes out of sight;
But the great and flashing magpie
He flies as poets might.)

T. P. Cameron Wilson
Killed in action, 1918

GETHSEMANE (1914–18)

The Garden called Gethsemane
   In Picardy it was,
And there the people came to see
   The English soldiers pass.

We used to pass – we used to pass
   Or halt, as it might be,
And ship our masks in case of gas
   Beyond Gethsemane.

The Garden called Gethsemane,
   It held a pretty lass,
But all the time she talked to me
   I prayed my cup might pass.
The officer sat on the chair,
   The men lay on the grass,
And all the time we halted there
   I prayed my cup might pass.

It didn't pass – it didn't pass –
  It didn't pass from me.
I drank it when we met the gas
  Beyond Gethsemane!

Rudyard Kipling

Going into the Line

At 3.15, No. 11 Platoon, 100 yards in rear of No. 10,
will move from Pommiers Redoubt.

                               So soon!
At 3.15. And would return here . . . when?
It didn't say. Who would return? P'raps all,
P'raps none. Then it had come at last!
It had come at last! his own stupendous hour,
Long waited, dreaded, almost hoped-for too,
When all else seemed the foolery of power;
It had come at last! and suddenly the world
Was sharply cut in two. On one side lay
A golden, dreamy, peaceful afternoon,
And on the other, men gone mad with fear,
A hell of noise and darkness, a Last Day
Daily enacted. Now good-bye to one
And to the other . . . well, acceptance: that
At least he'd give; many had gone with joy:
He loathed it from his very inmost soul.

The golden world! It lay just over there,
Peacefully dreaming. In its clear bright depths
Friends moved – he saw them going here and there,
Like thistledown above an August meadow:
Gently as in a gentle dream they moved,
Unagonized, unwrought, nor sad, nor proud,
Faces he loved to agony – and none
Could see, or know, or bid him well–adieu.
Blasphemous irony! To think how oft
On such a day a friend would hold his hand
Saying good-bye, though they would meet next day,
And now . . . He breathed his whole soul out,
Bidding it span the unbridged senseless miles
And glow about their thoughts in waves of love.

'Twas time already! Now? As soon as this?
Did his voice hold? How did he look to them?
Poor craven little crowd of human mites!
Now they were crawling over the scarred cheese,
Silently going towards that roaring sea,
Each thinking his own thought, craving perhaps
A body that would fail, or with set teeth
Pitting a human will against the world.
Now every step seemed an eternity:

Each stretch of earth unreachable until it lay
Behind and a stretch longer lay beyond.
Would it never be ended? Crumbling earth,
Dry with the cracks of earthquake, dumbly showed
Death had just trodden there – and there he lay,
Foully deformed in what was once a man.
'Lo! as these are, so shalt thou be', he thought,
Shuddered: then thrilled almost to ecstasy,
As one from hell delivered up to heaven.

How slow they moved in front! Yes, slower still.
Then we must stop: we were not eighty yards.
But to stop here – to wait for it! Oh no!
Backward or forward, anything but not stop –
Not stand and wait! There's no alternative.
And now he rasps out, 'Halt!' They stand and curse,
Eyes furtive, fingers moving senselessly.
There comes a roar nearer and louder till
His head is bursting with noise and the earth shakes.
'A bloody near one, that!' and 'What the hell
Are we stuck here for?' come with sudden growls.
He moves without a word, and on they trudge.
So near! Yet nothing! Then how long? How long? . . .

And slowly in his overheated mind
Peace like a river through the desert flows,
And sweetness wells and overflows in streams
That reach the farthest friend in memory.
Peace now, and dear delight in serving these,
These poor sheep, driven innocent to death:
Peace undisturbed, though the poor senses jump,
And horror catches at the heart as when
Death unsuspected flaunts his grisly hand
Under the very eye of quietness:
Peace, peace with all, even the enemy,
Compassion for them deep as for his own:
Quietness now amid the thunderous noise,
And sweet elation in the grave of gloom.

Max Plowman
The Somme, August 1916

SPRING OFFENSIVE

Halted against the shade of a last hill,
They fed, and, lying easy, were at ease
And, finding comfortable chests and knees
Carelessly slept. But many there stood still
To face the stark, blank sky beyond the ridge,
Knowing their feet had come to the end of the world.

Marvelling they stood, and watched the long grass
   swirled
By the May breeze, murmurous with wasp and midge,
For though the summer oozed into their veins
Like the injected drug for their bones' pains,
Sharp on their souls hung the imminent line of grass,
Fearfully flashed the sky's mysterious glass.

Hour after hour they ponder the warm field —
And the far valley behind, where the buttercups
Had blessed with gold their slow boots coming up,
Where even the little brambles would not yield,
But clutched and clung to them like sorrowing hands;
They breathe like trees unstirred.

Till like a cold gust thrilled the little word
At which each body and its soul begird
And tighten them for battle. No alarms
Of bugles, no high flags, no clamorous haste —
Only a lift and flare of eyes that faced
The sun, like a friend with whom their love is done.
O larger shone that smile against the sun, —
Mightier than his whose bounty these have spurned.

So, soon they topped the hill, and raced together
Over an open stretch of herb and heather
Exposed. And instantly the whole sky burned
With fury against them; and soft sudden cups
Opened in thousands for their blood; and the green
    slopes
Chasmed and steepened sheer to infinite space.

Of them who running on that last high place
Leapt to swift unseen bullets, or went up
On the hot blast and fury of hell's upsurge,
Or plunged and fell away past this world's verge,
Some say God caught them even before they fell.

But what say such as from existence' brink
Ventured but drave too swift to sink.
The few who rushed in the body to enter hell,
And there out-fiending all its fiends and flames
With superhuman inhumanities,
Long-famous glories, immemorial shames —
And crawling slowly back, have by degrees
Regained cool peaceful air in wonder —
Why speak they not of comrades that went under?

Wilfred Owen

In Memoriam

(Private D. Sutherland, killed in action in the
German trench, 16 May 1916, and the others
who died)

So you were David's father,
And he was your only son,
And the new-cut peats are rotting
And the work is left undone,
Because of an old man weeping,
Just an old man in pain,
For David, his son David,
That will not come again.

Oh, the letters he wrote you,
And I can see them still,
Not a word of the fighting
But just the sheep on the hill
And how you should get the crops in
Ere the year get stormier,
And the Bosches have got his body,
And I was his officer.

You were only David's father,
But I had fifty sons
When we went up in the evening
Under the arch of the guns,
And we came back at twilight –
O God! I heard them call
To me for help and pity
That could not help at all.

Oh, never will I forget you,
My men that trusted me,
More my sons than your fathers',
For they could only see
The little helpless babies
And the young men in their pride.
They could not see you dying,
And hold you while you died.

Happy and young and gallant,
They saw their first-born go,
But not the strong limbs broken
And the beautiful men brought low,
The piteous writhing bodies,
They screamed 'Don't leave me, sir,'
For they were only your fathers
But I was your officer.

E. A. Mackintosh
Killed in action, 1916

In the Ambulance

Two rows of cabbages,
Two of curly-greens,
Two rows of early peas,
Two of kidney-beans.

That's what he keeps muttering,
Making such a song,
Keeping other chaps awake
The whole night long.

Both his legs are shot away,
And his head is light,
So he keeps on muttering
All the blessed night:

Two rows of cabbages,
Two of curly-greens,
Two rows of early peas,
Two of kidney-beans.

W. W. Gibson

FROM THE SOMME

In other days I sang of simple things,
    Of summer dawn, and summer noon and night,
The dewy grass, the dew-wet fairy rings,
        The larks long golden flight.

Deep in the forest I made melody
    While squirrels cracked their hazel nuts on high,
Or I would cross the wet sand to the sea
        And sing to sea and sky.

When came the silvered silence of the night
    I stole to casements over scented lawns,
And softly sang of love and love's delight
        To mute white marble fauns.

Oft in the tavern parlour I would sing
    Of morning sun upon the mountain vine,
And, calling for a chorus, sweep the string
        In praise of good red wine.

I played with all the toys the gods provide,
    I sang my songs and made glad holiday.
Now I have cast my broken toys aside
        And flung my lute away.

A singer once, I now am fain to weep.
  Within my soul I feel strange music swell,
Vast chants of tragedy too deep – too deep
    For my poor lips to tell.

Leslie Coulson
Killed in action, 1916

IN FLANDERS FIELDS

In Flanders fields the poppies blow
Between the crosses, row on row,
   That mark our place; and in the sky
   The larks, still bravely singing, fly
Scarce heard amid the guns below.

We are the Dead. Short days ago
We lived, felt dawn, saw sunset glow,
   Loved and were loved, and now we lie
      In Flanders fields.

Take up our quarrel with the foe:
To you from failing hands we throw
   The torch; be yours to hold it high.
   If ye break faith with us who die
We shall not sleep, though poppies grow
      In Flanders fields.

John McCrae

AN IRISH AIRMAN FORESEES HIS DEATH

I know that I shall meet my fate
Somewhere among the clouds above;
Those that I fight I do not hate,
Those that I guard I do not love;
My country is Kiltartan Cross,
My countrymen Kiltartan's poor,
No likely end could bring them loss
Or leave them happier than before.
Nor law, nor duty bade me fight,
Nor public men, nor cheering crowds,

A lonely impulse of delight
Drove to this tumult in the clouds;
I balanced all, brought all to mind,
The years to come seemed waste of breath,
A waste of breath the years behind
In balance with this life, this death.

W. B. Yeats

EVERYONE SANG

Everyone suddenly burst out singing;
And I was filled with such delight
As prisoned birds must find in freedom,
Winging wildly across the white
Orchards and dark-green fields; on—on—and out
  of sight.

Everyone's voice was suddenly lifted;
And beauty came like the setting sun:
My heart was shaken with tears; and horror
Drifted away . . . O, but Everyone
Was a bird; and the song was wordless; the singing
  will never be done.

Siegfried Sassoon

1916 Seen from 1921

Tired with dull grief, grown old before my day,
I sit in solitude and only hear
Long silent laughters, murmurings of dismay,
The lost intensities of hope and fear;
In those old marshes yet the rifles lie,
On the thin breastwork flutter the grey rags,
The very books I read are there – and I
Dead as the men I loved, wait while life drags

Its wounded length from those sad streets of war
Into green places here, that were my own;
But now what once was mine is mine no more,
I seek such neighbours here and I find none.
With such strong gentleness and tireless will
Those ruined houses seared themselves in me,
Passionate I look for their dumb story still,
And the charred stub outspeaks the living tree.

I rise up at the singing of a bird
And scarcely knowing slink along the lane,
I dare not give a soul a look or word
Where all have homes and none's at home in vain:
Deep red the rose burned in the grim redoubt,
The self-sown wheat around was like a flood,
In the hot path the lizard lolled time out,
The saints in broken shrines were bright as blood.

Sweet Mary's shrine between the sycamores!
There we would go, my friend of friends and I,
And snatch long moments from the grudging wars,
Whose dark made light intense to see them by.
Shrewd bit the morning fog, the whining shots
Spun from the wrangling wire; then in warm swoon
The sun hushed all but the cool orchard plots,
We crept in the tall grass and slept till noon.

Edmund Blunden

The Lament of the Demobilized

'Four years,' some say consolingly. 'Oh well,
What's that? You're young. And then it must have
  been
A very fine experience for you!'
And they forget
How others stayed behind and just got on—
Got on the better since we were away.
And we came home and found
They had achieved, and men revered their names,
But never mentioned ours;
And no one talked heroics now, and we
Must just go back and start again once more.
'You threw four years into the melting-pot—
Did you indeed!' these others cry. 'Oh well,
The more fool you!'
And we're beginning to agree with them.

Vera Brittain

RECONCILIATION

When you are standing at your hero's grave,
Or near some homeless village where he died,
Remember, through your heart's rekindling pride,
The German soldiers who were loyal and brave.

Men fought like brutes; and hideous things were
    done,
And you have nourished hatred harsh and blind.
But in that Golgotha perhaps you'll find
The mothers of the men who killed your son.

Siegfried Sassoon
November 1918

ELEGY IN A COUNTRY CHURCHYARD

The men that worked for England
They have their graves at home:
And bees and birds of England
About the cross can roam.

But they that fought for England,
Following a falling star,
Alas, alas for England
They have their graves afar.

And they that rule in England,
In stately conclave met,
Alas, alas for England
They have no graves as yet.

G. K. Chesterton
Published in 1922

AFTERMATH

Have you forgotten yet? . . .
For the world's events have rumbled on since those
gagged days,
Like traffic checked while at the crossing of city-
ways:
And the haunted gap in your mind has filled with
thoughts that flow
Like clouds in the lit heaven of life; and you're a man
reprieved to go,
Taking your peaceful share of Time, with joy to
spare.
*But the past is just the same—and War's a bloody
game . . .*
Have you forgotten yet? . . .
*Look down, and swear by the slain of the War that you'll
never forget.*

Do you remember the dark months you held the
sector at Mametz?
The nights you watched and wired and dug and piled
sandbags on parapets?

Do you remember the rats; and the stench
Of corpses rotting in front of the front-line trench—
And dawn coming, dirty-white, and chill with a
    hopeless rain?
Do you ever stop and ask, 'Is it all going to happen
    again?'

Do you remember that hour of din before the
    attack—
And the anger, the blind compassion that seized and
    shook you
As you peered at the doomed and haggard faces of
    your men?
Do you remember the stretcher-cases lurching back
With dying eyes and lolling heads—those ashen-grey
Masks of the lads who once were keen and kind
    and gay?

Have you forgotten yet? . . .
*Look up, and swear by the green of the spring that you'll
    never forget.*

Siegfried Sassoon

Index of First Lines

INDEX OF POETS

Acknowledgements

The compiler and publisher wish to thank the following for permission to use copyright material:

Blunden, Edmund, 'Vlamertinghe: Passing the Château, July, 1917', 'Two Voices' and '1916 Seen from 1921', by permission of David Higham Associates Ltd on behalf of the author; **Brittain, Vera**, 'Perhaps', 'To My Brother' and 'The Lament of the Demobilized', included by permission of Mark Bostridge and T. J. Britain-Catlin, literary executors for the Vera Brittain estate 1970; **Daryush, Elizabeth**, 'Flanders Fields', from *Selected Poems*, by permission of Carcanet Press Limited; **Farjeon, Eleanor**, 'Easter Monday', by permission of David Higham Associates Ltd on behalf of the author; **Gordon Keown, Anna**, 'Reported Missing', by kind permission of Jennifer Gosse; **Herbert, A.P**, 'Beaucourt Revisited', by permission of A. P. Watt at United Agents on behalf of the executors of the estate of Jocelyn Herbert, M. T. Perkins and Polly M. V. R. Perkins; **Letts, Winifred**, 'The Deserter', from *Halloween and Poems of the War*, published 1916 by Smith, Elder and Co.; **Macaulay, Rose**, 'Many Sisters to Many Brothers' and 'Picnic', by kind permission of The Society of Authors as the literary representative of the estate of Rose Macaulay; **Nichols, Robert**, 'Noon', by kind permission of Mr and Mrs William Charlton; **Postgate Cole, Margaret**, 'The Falling Leaves', by permission of David Higham Associates Ltd on behalf of the author; **Sassoon, Siegfried**, 'Base Details', 'In the Church of St Ouen', 'The Dug-out', 'Everyone Sang', 'Reconciliation' and 'Aftermath' copyright Siegfried Sassoon, by kind permission of the Estate of George Sassoon; **Williams, I. A.**, 'From a Flemish Graveyard', by kind permission of Edward Williams.

Every effort has been made to trace the copyright holders, but if any have been inadvertently overlooked the publisher will be pleased to make the necessary arrangement at the first opportunity.